WHEN THE DRAGON HATCHED

WHEN THE DRAGON HATCHED

KAYLA McDANIEL

When the Dragon Hatched
© 2025 Kayla McDaniel
Cover Art © 2025 Kayla McDaniel
ISBN: 979-8-9987811-5-5

Published by Youth Writer's Press
Colton, California
youthwriterspress.com

First Edition, 2025

To request permissions, you may contact the Publisher at
info@youthwriterscamp.com

Printed in the United States of America.

Cover design by Kayla McDaniel & Emily Anne Evans
Layout design by Emily Anne Evans / Photon Moment LLC

To those who helped me realize that my emotions are not a dragon to fear or tame, but instead, is a part of me to accept and collaborate with.

Contents

FOREWORD

From the moment Kayla McDaniel first put pen to paper, it was clear she had a gift for seeing the world in ways that most of us overlook. Now, as a senior in high school, Kayla has transformed that gift into this beautiful collection of poetry—a work that reflects both her talent and her heart.

This book was born from a place of deep personal loss. After the heartbreaking passing of a close friend, Kayla turned to writing as a way to process the pain, confusion, and grief that followed. What began as a quiet outlet became a powerful voice—one that carried her through sorrow, reflection, healing, and hope.

Her poetry is a map of that emotional journey. You'll find rawness and tenderness, anger and acceptance, stillness and growth. Each piece marks a moment in her transition—from mourning to meaning, from silence to expression.

It is my honor to introduce you to the poetry of Kayla McDaniel, a writer whose words are as brave as they are beautiful. May her voice move you, as it has moved all of us who've watched her grow—not only as a student, but as an artist, and as a person.

— *Proud Parents, April and Matthew McDaniel*

WHEN THE DRAGON HATCHED

THE EGG

"Who are you?"
Is a loaded question.
A million different answers
Not one elaborate enough
To satisfy
The complexity of their inquiry.
The mind picks up and runs off
With every idea, emotion, and phrase
But are those thoughts who I am?

I am a human being,
Who lives and breathes.
I am a woman,
Who monthly bleeds.
I can feel and move and see and hear.
I can speak, if only through a filter.

I can call myself kind or passionate
I'd give up my heart,
My strength,
So others feast
And don't go hungry.
But I haven't ate.

My dragon hasn't hatched.

I'd call myself selfless,
But sometimes that's not true.

I have wants and desires.
I'm human too.
I still feel the hunger
Though food may be sparse.
My dragon is tapping,
Tap, tapping the shell of its cage
And then stops.
I never take more than they willingly give.

I'd like to believe I'm intelligent.
I am told all the time.
I receive gifts of greatness,
Yet question if I am great,
Or just my gifts.
Truly who am I?
I am nothing if not myself.
I cannot be another person.
I can only be myself.
Except for the dragon who lives as a part of me,
Locked away by fear of rejection,
Sealed in a tomb of shell because of what?
One person's mouth.
Reverted to nothing more than an egg
Docile, weak, laying in wait, i'll
Hope
And fear
The day it hatches.

My Heart Dragon

Inside me,
A dragon lay dormant.
Awoken in torment,
Rages till it's contained.
Looks like it finally hatched.

The dragon is defensive,
It protects its own.
It sets the ground on fire,
And burns all of its foes
Once angered,
The dragon doesn't stop,
It continues and continues
Until there's nothing that's not lost
It burns from the inside,
It rots,
It festers,
It lies and waits
For for the cage to settle,
To hide,
But it doesn't.

The dragon is obedient to the whims of the mind.
The mind doesn't stop,
So neither does the dragon.
The heart they share is pounding rapidly.
Beating, beating,
Mourning the loss,

Feeling lines that were crossed,
Catching the pieces,
Before their heart grows moss.

The dragon is out of control.
It stretches the heart,
It strains its wings,
The space is closing in,
Closing tighter and tighter.
The dragon is screaming in tandem with the heart:
"MAKE IT STOP!"

Our heart feels like it's bursting.
But my dragon is clawing the inside
And I'm clawing from outside.
"Make it stop, please."
The mind finally agrees.
The cage comes down,
The dragon settles to the ground,
The fires burn out,
And the mind becomes too loud,
But it's numb.
The dragon, my heart,
Becomes cold and lifeless.
Until the spark reignites its flame
And it's released from its cage.
To ravage and pain,
Like the first time never happened.

WHEN THE DRAGON HATCHED

When the dragon hatched
It wasn't clean,
There was blood and scales all over the scene.
The dragon broke from its shell,
As it was old enough to escape hell
Just to find another cell.

The dragon, *my dragon*,
Originally hatched from the thrash
Of waves of water.
Though it wasn't water, was it?
Tears sound more accurate.
I lost a person who meant the world to me.
And she was who I wanted to be.

Kind like the arms that held me when I cried,
Impressively forgiving of all my wrongdoings,
Mans up, stands up, was always on my side,
Made me smile and laugh every chance she had, and
Incredibly strong, she would never hide.

My dragon hatched the day hers died.
I couldn't stop the shell from cracking.
I couldn't stop the fire burning.
I couldn't stop my heart from breaking.

The dragon wanted to burn
And I let it burn.
But not the others I see,
I didn't want them to know,
So I told it to burn me
And it did as it was told.
My mind was disconnected,
Stuck in the casket with her.
While my heart remained behind,
The dragon was left to unwind
And it burned till I became blind.

I thought it would scar me forever.
I thought i'd have to live with the fear and guilt
Forever.
Because I never cared to heal the scars,
The burns.
Because the dragon was telling me,
I wouldn't have to bother.

Death felt all but necessary
Face to face with my own adversary:
My heart and my mind.
Each their own ally.
Each their own enemy.
My body became no man's land.
And no one could lend a hand.

I was alone,
Locked in the dark with no key,
Stuck in the grief like tar
I had no peace
And no piece of my heart was complete
That left me obsolete,
Under defeat,
I can never go back
To the days before I was weak.
So now I say,
Dear me,
Be who *she'd* want you to be.

A Dragon Contained

The dragon inside
was one I thought to be my enemy.
It burned down my ships,
And It hid faced with superiority.
It defended its blazing ground,
Not realizing
That there was no one left around.
That it was burning nothing but itself
And me.

I was burned till I was ill,
But I had had enough.
I had grown more in mind's will,
Then in height or gruff.

In a moment of my will,
A want that the dragon couldn't fill,
I let my mind reign it to still,
Let my thoughts muzzle its sharp mouth,
Let my fear shackle it to the cold ground.

Though,
My dragon has hatched.
I cannot rewind the past.
It cannot crawl back into its shell,
Cannot revert back to being cells.

But I can restrain it.
I can train it.
"My mind can tame the beast!"
I stated it.

The dragon lay anxious,
Scared of what comes next.
I gave the dragon something to fear:
My mind the only thing to hear.
I acted on every thought,
And thought too much.
Veering off the side
Of the waves that became my mind.

Mind, no heart on the side.
Thoughts with no dragon.
Water over fire.
I was drowning rather than burning.
Trapped in a cage of my design.
My *Mind's* design.

I used to be raging,
Now I am reigned.
I refrain from outlashing.
Tangled in logic.
Contained,
But no longer sane.

When Failure Comes Knocking

Bum Bump. Bum Bump.

The echoes in my chest
Heave and ho
As I grapple with the rest
Of the ideas
The thoughts like a pest
In my head.
I'm not made of steel.

Bum Bump, Bum Bump

My porcelain frame is cracking,
Breaking.
What if I am caught slacking?
What if I'm lacking?
What if I can't catch myself
Before the pieces become plaque in—

Bum Bump Bum Bump

My heart.
It's hurting.
My mind is racing.
I am not a racecar.
I am not fast enough.
Why do I fear the seconds?

Bum Bump Bum—

The seconds move faster, faster.
Running.
Run away!
Why do I fear you?

Bum Bump—

Why are you always here?
The thoughts,
The "what if's?"

Bum Bu—

Go away!
I don't need you here!

Bum—

WHY MUST I FEAR MY FAILURE?

Bum
Bump
Bum
Bump
Bum
Bump

Why focus on the
"If I fail?"

Bum Bump

My heart feels like a bomb,
Counting the seconds.
Second place
Doesn't seem so bad anymore.

Bum bump bum bump

I know my own strengths.
I know I can be great
No, I *am* great.
Great at being me,
The greatest pretender,
But the best at being me.

Bum Bump. Bum Bump

I may not get first every time
But I sure will try.
I may not say the best rhyme
But I sure will try.
I may not read the signs
But I sure will try.
And that is enough.

I am not afraid of failure,
I just read between the lines.

THE COMPROMISE

Shackled to the ground,
Stuck in the cage,
Ashes blow like dust to the wind.
The dragon is silent;
Tamed by my will.
It will not rage again.
It will not burn me again.

Are you happy?
The voice comes from within.

"I no longer have to deal with your *attitude*.
You burned me,
My friends have left me,
But now you burn no longer.
You are doomed to be locked up forever
By my hand. By *my* will."

Are you happy?
The dragon asks again.

"Why do you ask me a question only you know?
My mind is apart but I reap what you sow.
We are separate beings connected in consequence.
But what I feel can't be pushed off as a pretense.
What I feel is intense and wrong
Can't you see this has gone on too long?"

Are you–?

"Stop asking me that!
You are nothing!
Face the facts!
You have failed!
I see your cracks!
I'm relieved!
I should be–"

Happy?

I should be happy,
But I feel…

Nothing.
Not without me.

…
Nothing.

My resolve begins to melt
As the shackles melt with it.
Why did I fear the very life I lit?
Why did I turn my heart into a pit
And threw away my feelings
Pretending they weren't felt?

It seemed like a great vision
Standing far from the screen,
But now that it's here,

It no longer looks like a dream.
I'm not whole without my dragon in toll.
I cannot misuse and abuse
For amusement.
That's the truth.
Power is fleeting.
Replaced by time with guilt.

"Im sorry."
My voice sounds like silt,
Smooth but smothered.

You fear what you cannot tame,
You bury beneath the lame
But you are not innocent,
I suffered at your hands,
And I became the loser
Forced to play your game.
I was the pawn you placed to die.
But I am the half that doesn't lie.
I feel only truth.
So I am sorry too.

We both made mistakes,
Though we both felt justified.
We thought for ourselves,
And not for each other's lives.
But just like an old friend,
We will talk and compromise.

THE FINE LINE

I often dream of a non-reality
Where everything was perfect,
My mind and body were clean
Gleaming with health
Like the sunrise on the sea,
Excited for the new day,
Good news to feed my brain.
My thought train chugging
Strong till the end of the stay.

But my bedsheets are heavy
My mind is heady
Like I'm filled with lead.
I dont think i'm ready
To wake.
Im unsteady on my feet
"Just make it through the day"
And then return to your bed, see.

My favorites are arranged
Warm waffles, cold strawberries,
And orange juice tang.
This isn't strange.
I eat my fill.
Not worried of the weight I'll gain
Or the calories to slain.
Grateful for every bite.
Living life outside the pain.

"Life is great"
But I lay as they pass by.
There's a great dead bird
Lying in the street.
A crow nonetheless.
Ironic to see Death die.
Felled by man.
The people all around us lie,
"They didn't have the strength to fly"
When did the bird become I?
Why?

Every day I walk a fine line.
Wake up alive
Or feel dead inside.
My center of gravity shifts and changes,
Constantly moving back and forth on ranges.
Should I go out
Or stay in and pout?
Should I be loud
Or not make a sound?
Can I eat even if it's unhealthy?
Can I live and truly be me?

Swimming and Drowning

The wolves whistle on the wind.
The colors of the ocean as it bends and turn
Flowing down, down, down
Down.
Gravity pulling at the hems and seams,
Till it forms a new stream.
One of less resistance.
Is the water dead or alive?

The violation that you feel,
Discarded to the wind.
You can't reject the flow of water,
Even as it drowns you alive.
Does it matter if it's dead or alive?
Dead or Alive?

Am I alive?
If I just lay and let the water ravage me?
Am I alive?
I sure feel dead.
Will I ever want to swim again,
Knowing what happened the first time
I trusted nature?
I didn't drown.
I'm still alive.

But the memory drowns my brain
Taking up space
With its salty water
That filled my face.

Why did I trust the water?
Maybe because I'm around it every day.
I didn't think twice to check.
Check if this water was the same I'd always known.
The water that nourished me.
The water that kept me alive.
Alive.
I am still alive.
But never the same.
I'll never look at *water* the same way again.
I'm still alive.
But some part of me died.

Two Halves of the Same Whole

Can I speak?
I am lightheaded and dizzy.
Can I show my opinion
or will it be lost in the sea
Of the voices
Of the loud
And the healthy.
Healthy enough to criticize,
To anger
To hurt.
I sit in my thoughts
as they fester
to their own being.
One not my own.
Apart.
With its own thoughts.
Ones I cannot speak
Or sympathize.
I bubble and boil over
While this being radiates cool,
Like mint and sunscreen.
I am the sunburn,
Continuing deeper,
Burning hot under my skin
Until illness results as the flame to the kindling.
It's hot and I'm dizzy.

Spinning,
Round and round.
The world is round but they argue that too.
Can I speak?
I cannot move.
My chest constricting
Burning.
Hurting.

I look at her with envy.
The girl of cool shade and snow.
I look at her and wish
That she were burning too.
I look at my other half,
The better half,
And wonder when she will become me.

QUESTIONS AND ANSWERS

Life is filled with questions and answers
"Hello, how are you?"
"Im tired, that's the truth."

The questions and answers
Slowly become more difficult.
"What is 9+8?"
"17"

The questions and answers
Slowly become more intricate.
"How are you feeling?
Tell me where it hurts."
"Well sir, my heart hurts.
I think it might be broken."

The questions and answers
Slowly become more automated.
"Hello, how are you?
What's your name?"
"Im good.
My name is Kayla.
And you?"

The questions and answers
Slowly become more internal.
"What was his birthday?"
"Oh, right. December 30th."

The questions and answers
Slowly become more dark.
"Why did I do that?
I didn't mean to hurt them."
"I need to distance.
Make sure I don't hurt them again."

The questions and answers
Slowly become just questions.
"What am I doing here?
Why am I not pretty?
Why did I do that?
Why do I always mess up?
When can I go home?
Why am I a failure?"

The questions and questions
Received only one simple answer:
"Give up."

But before I gave up,
I received a different answer.
One not from me.
One in the form of a question.

"Why are you so beautiful?"

And instead of answering,
I just sat and stared.
For once,
I couldn't find a good answer.

"Why are you so kind?
Why are you so silly?
Why do you hide your beautiful smile?
Why are you stressed, baby?
Why don't you get some rest, sweetheart?
Why are you crying?"

All my questions suddenly had answers.
Not difficult,
Not intricate,
Not automated,
Not internal,
Not dark answers.
Real, truthful answers.
And my heart no longer questioned
"Why?"

OTHER WORKS BY THE AUTHOR

- - - - - - - - - - - - - - - - - - -

Written during a time of turmoil.
Read during a time of peace.
Shared for the awareness of others.
Each a mark in my history.
-K.M.

CONDITIONAL GREATNESS

This poem explores the fluctuating feeling of greatness and the expectation that comes with being great.

Conditional greatness.
A condition to greatness.
Why am I great one moment
And worse the next?
Why do I find it easy today
And difficult tomorrow?
Why can I explain my thoughts
But never write them clearly?
Why can I never see the deeper meaning?

Conditional greatness.
What are the conditions to greatness?
Must I roar with the voice of a bird?
Must I run with the legs of a snake?
Must I do the unobtainable?
Do what cannot be done?
Face the music that is only notes
Written on the page?
But I'm expected to hear it.
I cannot hear the illusory music
from that ink on the page.
All I see is ink
Nothing of greatness to me.

Conditional greatness.
The condition of greatness
Is to have an eye that can see the invisible,
Ears that hear the unsaid,
And a mouth that speaks what others think.

JUST THE RED THAT I SEE

This poem displays the struggles I've felt with being a
woman during my monthly period. This poem was written at
two in the morning.

Whenever I see red,
My body starts to shake with emotion I shouldn't feel
but emotion I do.
My face rips apart,
and a smile comes out.
This is not me, it's just the red I see.
My eyes water and my dog is concerned,
or frightened.
Every small thing is big,
just as every big thing is small.
Like the red that I feel.
No sleep, can't eat, no memory of why,
but it is still,
the red that I see.
Powerful but weak, blunt but sharp,
The worst that could happen
is the red to be gone
And that cannot be because it's always
Just the red that I see.
On my feet.
In my head.
In my mouth.
Not dead, but close.
Walking, bleeding flesh with a full but empty glass.
A glass of red, because that's all I'll see.

At least for the while,
I am the red
and the red is me.
And that's all I'll ever be.
Just the red that I see.
The red that I bleed, monthly.

WHEN ME AND MY FEARS TAKE FLIGHT

This poem, while short, sums up my feelings associated with fear. Fear acts so quickly when a situation arises. I learned the hard way that fear doesn't cancel out fear.

When me and my fears take flight
I won't be around long enough to fear

After all…

You have to fall in order to fly
And to fly you need wings
But you fear those too
So you never actually fly,

You just die.

A Cool Glass of Water

This poem is about mistakes and acceptance, hasty decisions and feeling failure constantly. I felt that I could never gain this person's acceptance back ever again.

Acceptance is like
A cool glass of water
On a hot sunny day
After work.
Refreshing and promising
Of more to come
You drink more and more
And want for more and more
You try to get more
But your cup breaks
1 step forward
2 steps back...
Always.
Two.
Steps.
Back.
Acceptance feels good when you receive it,
But on a cold day
When you're splashed with cold water,
It's a shock.
You were once accepted but now you're not.
What changed?
Your mistakes you thought you left in the past
1 step forward, 2 steps back.

You broke your cup, though you tried to fix it
You put water back in and hoped it would hold
1 step forward, 2 steps back.
Until the cup falls apart again
And the cool, refreshing water runs out
1 step forward, 2 steps back.
The cool water feels good after a long day,
But after you run and run and try and try
And you get no cool water,
You lose faith.
You broke your cup, you can't fix it.
Acceptance is a cool glass of water.
I can't drink from you ever again.

ACKNOWLEDGMENTS

Thank you to everyone in my life: the good who helped me improve and pushed me to put my poetry out into the world, and the bad who gave me a good story to tell.

Especially thank you to Brandon who gave me this wonderful opportunity to share my poems on this big of a level, I am still in shock of how wonderfully big this step is in my writing journey. Brandon and Shaniese, you have been wonderful leaders throughout this 10-week adventure and you have created a community of passionate writers that I am proud to call mine! You encouraged building community within our small group and I came out with a multitude of new friends! Thank you to Miss Stephanie who taught me many different positive ways to channel emotions and was just a joy to be around! I will miss our group mental health time! Special thank you to Ms Cati Porter from Inlandia Institute for reaching out and giving me this wonderful opportunity! By you supporting the Youth Writer's Camp, you not only give students the opportunity to explore career paths in writing but you also give students access to alternative ways to manage emotional stresses and learn coping skills. Thank you again!

Thank you to my family, Mom, Dad, and Colton. You guys were the first to suggest I get my poetry out into the world. I underestimated my skill but I was proven wrong. Now I have a published book of my poetry! I'm very grateful for you helping me take this step and listening to me practice performing. I love you guys lots!

To my extended family, Grandma, Grandpa, Oma, Uncle Hunter, GT, Laura, and others, thank you for being a part of my life. I'm happy with the family I was born into and I wouldn't exchange you for the world! I have so many wonderful family members that crafted me into the woman I am today. Grandma, you especially have been motivating me to share my story and poetry. I'll never be lost when I have a compass to guide me to my true North. I'm happy to tell you that I did it! I am a published author! I love all of you!

To my friends I've made along the way, you guys are awesome! I love sharing my poetry with you all and your feedback is always helpful! Thank you for being lights in my life and sticking with me! I appreciate all the time we spend together! #ClassOf2026.

To the Salmon family, thank you for giving me the chance to be in your life. Joy and LaVon, you two are like my second parents. You bring life into your house and are great parents to your wonderful kids. I see you both in them. Thank you for giving me a safe space when I needed it most and thank you for including me in your adventures! Caylinn, Cali, and Cici, you guys are so fun to be around! I see you guys as my little sisters and no one can convince me to look at it any other way! Thank you for being a part of my life! Cyle, you are the most fantastic ray of greatness I've ever seen. You inspired me to look at myself in a positive light where I had previously been avoiding in the dark. You encouraged positive thoughts and pulled me from the depths of my mind where I thought I was stuck. You taught me that I could speak my truth and I wouldn't be judged for it. I learned that I am more than my image, I am valued, and valuable. You never fail to make me smile and laugh and I am truly honored to call you mine. With all my imperfections, all my beauty, all my thoughts, and all my heart, I love you. I look forward to many more tomorrows with you, many more late night calls, many more teases, many more laughs, and much more of you. Cyle, you were the answer I didn't realize I needed. Thank you for making life beautiful!

Thank you to everyone else who has supported me in life and in this journey! My teachers especially!

Lastly, thank you to my aunt. Auntie Kimmi, I know you would be so proud of me. I have grown so much since the last time I saw you. Though I may not be the small girl I once was, I am now a proud woman. I strive to be the kind of woman you were, kind and a great role model. Looking back, you would have been sad at how I was turning the direction of my life back then. I made selfishly poor choices that I regret now. However, I believe that the process of falling and getting back up while trying to get somewhere, is better than walking to nowhere. I met people who made the journey easier and created a "somewhere" for me to go. Whenever I fell, I had someone to help me. I miss you still even though 4 years have passed. I look back at the pictures and remember the sleepovers we had and the cinnamon Cinderella waffles, the Halloween movie nights, your dog Athena, making the shoe boxes for Operation Christmas Child, and you staying with us during COVID. I started taking writing seriously after you passed. Now it has become a passion of mine. I hope that my story, my poetry, will inspire others to find "somewhere" to go to. I hope you are sitting in Heaven, smiling down on me and waiting for the day we are reunited. I love you and miss you.

Rest In Peace, Auntie Kimmi.

- -

youthwriterspress.com

A program of Youth Writer's Camp, Inc., Youth Writer's Press exists to create a safe space where young voices are heard, valued, and amplified. We are dedicated to producing and publishing work that allows youth to share their truths with the world. Our mission is to equip the next generation of writers with the resources, confidence, and platform to turn their stories into lasting works that resound far beyond the page.

youthwriterscamp.com

This book was created as part of Youth Writer's Camp, Inc., a nonprofit organization whose mission is to motivate communities to redefine hope for young people through mentoring, enrichment, and creativity.

In our workshops and programs, we blend literacy enrichment, social-emotional development, and creative entrepreneurship – using writing as a tool for healing, growth, and community connection.

Youth Writer's Camp Values:

COURAGE Creating the strength to face challenges with confidence.

RESILIENCE Creating the ability to bounce back and keep moving forward.

EMPATHY Creating connections by truly understanding others' feelings.

AUTHENTICITY Creating a space where you can be your true self without masks.

TRANSPARENCY Creating an atmosphere of openness and honesty, where vulnerability is valued.

ENTERPRISING Creating opportunities through innovation and a dynamic mindset.